Hug a
Tree

Written and Illustrated by
Deanna Sagaris

Halo
PUBLISHING
INTERNATIONAL

Halo Publishing International
7550 WIH-10 #800, PMB 2069,
San Antonio, TX 78229

First Edition, June 2024
ISBN: 978-1-63765-626-6
Library of Congress Control Number: 2024911362

Halo Publishing International is a self-publishing company that publishes adult fiction and non-fiction, children's literature, self-help, spiritual, and faith-based books. Do you have a book idea you would like us to consider publishing? Please visit www.halopublishing.com for more information.

To Peter, the best
and most passionate
professor out there.

Trees need **love**

From everyone they know

And if no one loves them

How will they **grow**?

Branch by **branch**

And leaf by **leaf**

Trees will sprout

Unless there's a **thief**!

12

Axes will **chop**

Bulldozers will **plow**

It's not fair to the **air**

So we must help now!

What can you do

Save Trees!

From the comfort
of your **home**

So you can **care** for trees

And let them not feel alone?

Try using **less paper**

And **recycling** more!

Maybe **borrow** a book

And then another four!

Let's come **together**

Hand in hand

And try really hard
To restore our **land**!

As you save the trees
They save you!

Now take a deep breath
And **hug a tree**, too!

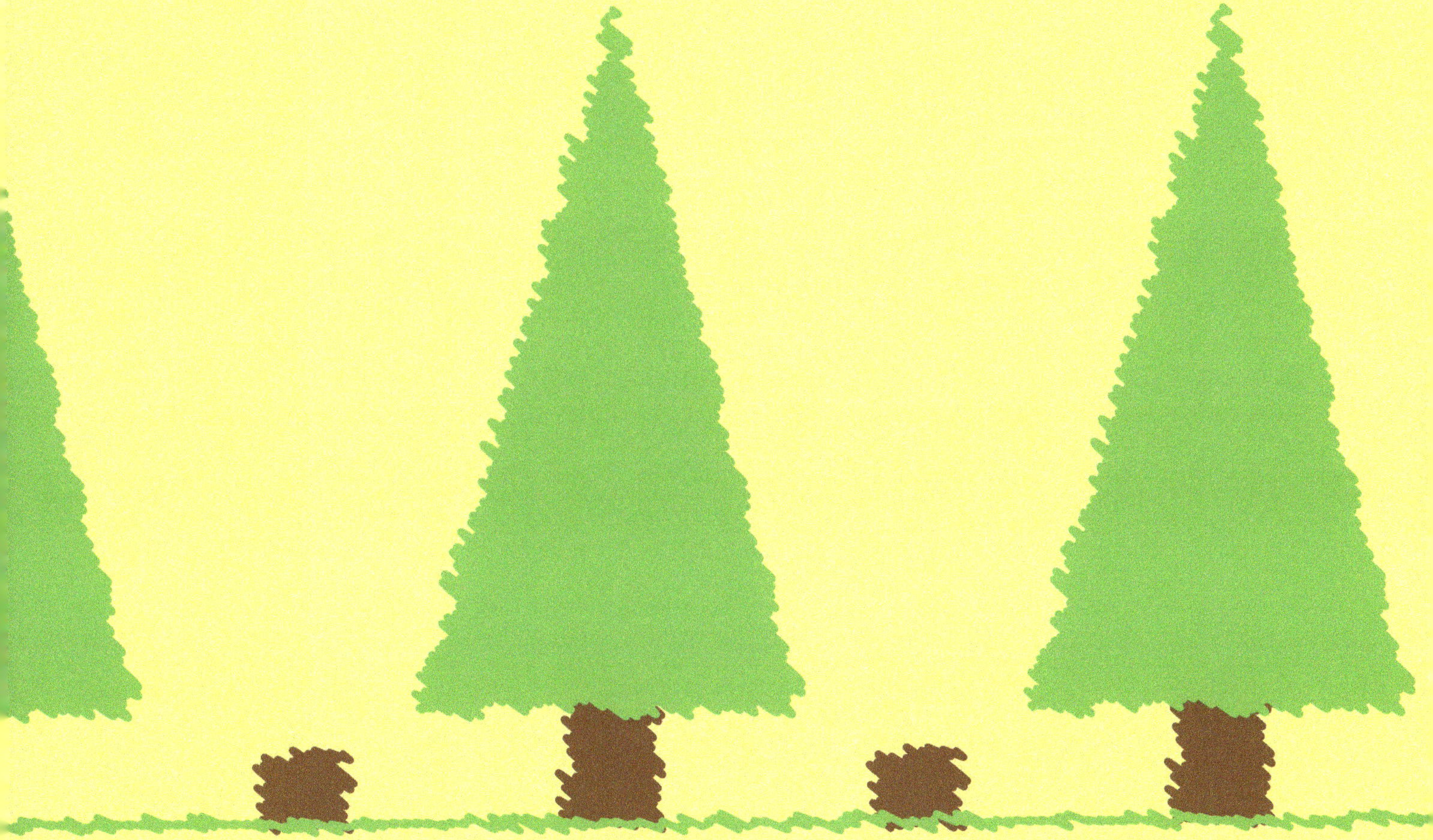

www.ingramcontent.com/pod-product-compliance
Lightning Source LLC
Chambersburg PA
CBHW060801150426
42813CB00058B/2782